Stitches from the Harvest

Stitches from the Harvest

Hand Embroidery Inspired by Autumn

Kathy Schmitz

Martingale®
Create with Confidence

Stitches from the Harvest: Hand Embroidery Inspired by Autumn
© 2017 by Kathy Schmitz

Martingale®
19021 120th Ave. NE, Ste. 102
Bothell, WA 98011-9511 USA
ShopMartingale.com

Printed in China
22 21 20 19 18 17   8 7 6 5 4 3 2 1

Library of Congress Cataloging-in-Publication Data
is available upon request.

ISBN: 978-1-60468-863-4

MISSION STATEMENT

We empower makers who use fabric and yarn to make life more enjoyable.

CREDITS

**PUBLISHER AND
CHIEF VISIONARY OFFICER**
Jennifer Erbe Keltner

CONTENT DIRECTOR
Karen Costello Soltys

DESIGN MANAGER
Adrienne Smitke

MANAGING EDITOR
Tina Cook

PRODUCTION MANAGER
Regina Girard

ACQUISITIONS EDITOR
Karen M. Burns

**COVER AND
INTERIOR DESIGNER**
Angie Hoogensen

TECHNICAL EDITOR
Ellen Pahl

PHOTOGRAPHER
Brent Kane

COPY EDITOR
Durby Peterson

ILLUSTRATOR
Anne Moscicki

DEDICATION
*To Mrs. Whitaker, my lovely neighbor who taught
me how to embroider when I was six years old*

Contents

in all things
Give Thanks

Introduction

Enjoying the crisp autumn air is one of the favorite memories of my youth. When the leaves began their colorful transformation to crimson, gold, and orange, I really felt at peace. These changes marked a new school year, and I have to admit, I loved going back to school as a kid. There was nothing like opening that new pack of crayons, wearing new kicks, and seeing old friends.

Right around the corner would be Halloween and then Thanksgiving—times to gather with friends and family, be thankful, and eat way too much good food and candy.

Many of the designs in this book came from a look back at my youth and those autumn days that were so special to me. From the time I was a little girl, I found acorns irresistible. So as I began these projects, I knew that the smooth nut and that cute nubby cap would have to be a big part of this book. One of the jack-o'-lanterns is even wearing an acorn cap as a hat! Oak leaves, blackberries, and woodland animals all gather throughout *Stitches from the Harvest,* adorning everything from a pillow to a table runner.

My days of coloring with crayons are well past me. Now I find great joy in painting with watercolors and "drawing" with a needle and beautiful thread. Won't you join me on a trip down memory lane and stitch some beautiful treasures of your own?

Autumn wears a CRIMSON crown
Kathy Schmitz

The MORNS are MEEKER than they were. The NUTS are getting BROWN; The berry's cheek is PLUMPER The Rose is Out of town

Three Jacks

*Three little jack-o'-lanterns will
brighten a spooky Halloween night.*

FINISHED SIZES
4", 5", AND 6" DIAMETER

Materials

Yardage is based on 42"-wide fabric.

⅜ yard of cream print for embroidery background

12" × 36" rectangle of lightweight batting

3 wooden embroidery hoops, 4", 5", and 6" diameter

Black craft paint and brush

Heavy-duty thread for gathering fabric

Embroidery Floss

Colors listed below are for The Gentle Art embroidery floss. For DMC equivalents, see page 75.

Moss (dark olive green) for dots and leaves

Picnic Basket (brown) for twigs and acorn hat

Raven (greenish black) for hats

Toffee (mustard gold) for star, dots, small acorn nut, and collar button

Tomato (orange) for pumpkins

Cutting

From the cream print, cut:

1 square, 12" × 12"

1 square, 11" × 11"

1 square, 10" × 10"

From the batting, cut:

1 square, 12" × 12"

1 square, 11" × 11"

1 square, 10" × 10"

Embroidering the Designs

1 Find the center of the cream background squares by gently finger-pressing each square in half vertically and horizontally.

2 Trace the embroidery pattern on page 11 for the 6" jack onto the 12" square. Trace the pattern on page 11 for the 5" jack onto the 11" square, and trace the pattern on page 12 for the 4" jack onto the 10" square.

3 Referring to "Embroidery Stitches" on page 76, use two strands of floss to embroider the designs, following the embroidery keys next to the patterns.

4 When the embroidery is complete, press well.

Finishing

1 Paint the outside hoops black, avoiding the metal pieces. Allow the paint to dry completely.

2 Place the appropriately sized inner hoop over each piece of embroidery, keeping the design centered. Draw a line around the outside of each hoop with a pencil or removable fabric marker as a guide for quilting.

3 Place the batting of the same size on the wrong side of each piece and then quilt as desired. I hand quilted a diagonal grid in the background with stitching lines ¼" apart. Avoid stitching over the embroidery.

4 Place a wooden outer hoop over each embroidery piece, keeping the design centered. Be sure to use the correct hoop size for each design. Trim each background square and batting into a circle, roughly 1½" beyond the edge of the hoop.

5 Thread a needle with heavy-duty thread and hand sew a basting stitch around each circle and batting, about ¼" to ½" from the edge.

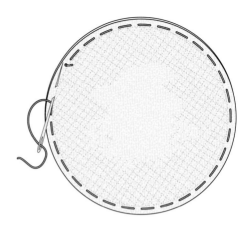

6 Place the embroidered and quilted pieces over the interior ring of the hoop with the design centered. Secure it in place with the outer hoop. Draw the ends of the basting stitches to gather the excess fabric on the back of the hoops. Tie a secure knot.

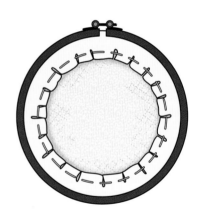

6" Jack

5" Jack

Embroidery key

- - - - - Backstitch

⊔⊔⊔⊔ Blanket stitch

>>>> Fern stitch

● French knot

– – – Running stitch

—— Stem stitch

— Straight stitch

4" Jack

Embroidery key

------- Backstitch

● French knot

– – – Running stitch

——— Stem stitch

— Straight stitch

Autumn Sheaf
Needle Keeper

*Your needles and threads have a cozy home
far away from the disarray of tangles and knots
in this folded needle-and-thread keeper.*

FINISHED SIZE
4½" × 4¼" CLOSED; 4½" × 17" OPEN

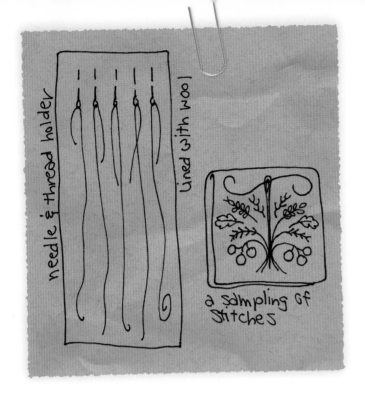

Embroidery Floss

Colors listed below are for The Gentle Art embroidery floss. For DMC equivalents, see page 75.

Autumn Leaves (yellow gold) for wheatear-stitch stalks

Moss (dark olive green) for large berry stems, oak leaves, and stems

Mulberry (dark brown red) for French knots and feather-stitch stalks

Old Hickory (brown gold) for fly-stitch stalks

Raven (greenish black) for thread, sheaf ties, and curved stitches

Ruby Slipper (rosy red) for large berries

Tin Bucket (blue gray) for needles

Materials

8" × 20" rectangle of cream print for exterior

5" × 20" rectangle of gold wool for interior

1⅜ yards of 1¼"-wide green rickrack (size #17)

1 snap, size #3

Fabric marker or permanent pen

Cardstock or other template material

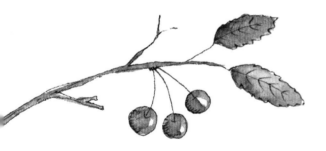

Embroidering the Design

1 Make a template from cardstock using the curve pattern on page 17.

2 Referring to the placement guide on page 15, draw two parallel lines, 5" apart, along the 20" length of the cream rectangle to mark the sides of the project. Draw a line 1" from and parallel to one 8" end to create the square end. From this line, measure down 17½" to mark the bottom of the curved edge. Mark the curved end of the project using the template. These will be the cutting lines after you stitch the embroidery, so use a marker that will not disappear when ironed.

3 Trace the sheaf embroidery pattern on page 17 so that it's centered side to side and the point of the needle is 1" from the bottom of the curve. Trace the needle-and-thread design so that the top of the thread is ½" from the top line and the point of the needle is ¾" from the left-side line.

4 Mark sewing lines ½" apart using the curve template. You should have 21 curved lines, not counting the needle-and-thread design at the square end.

5 Referring to "Embroidery Stitches" on page 76, use two strands of floss to embroider the designs, following the embroidery key next to the pattern. Stitch the sheaf ties last.

6 When the embroidery is complete, press well. Cut on the drawn cutting lines so that the piece measures 5" × 17½". Do not trim the curved edge yet.

Referring to "Embroidery Stitches" on page 76,

Stay inside the Lines

Keep all stitches inside the drawn cutting lines so that they won't be cut off later.

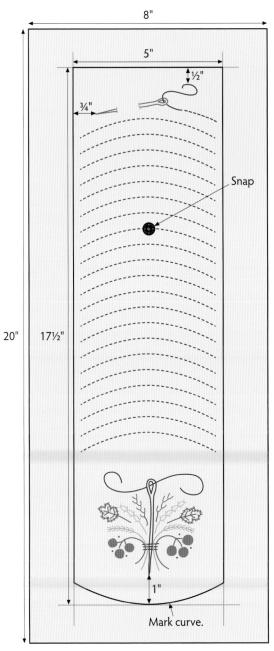

Placement guide

8"

5"

½"

¾"

Snap

20"

17½"

1"

Mark curve.

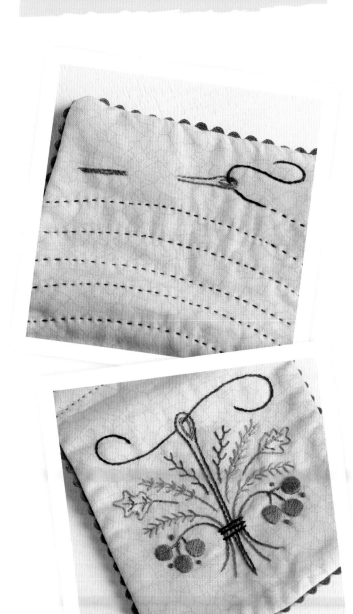

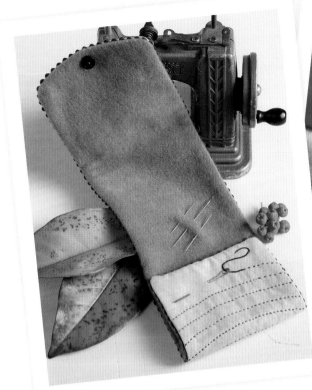

Assembling the Needle Keeper

1 Starting at the top-left corner, baste the rickrack to the right side of the project, a scant ¼" from the edge of the fabric, stitching through the center of the rickrack.

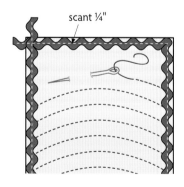

scant ¼"

2 Place the wool on the right side of the embroidery project and align the sides. There will be extra wool along the top and bottom; leave most of the excess along the straight end. Pin in place and sew together along the long sides and the curved end using a ¼" seam allowance. Do not sew across the straight end.

3 Trim away the excess wool at the curved end. Clip the corners and turn the piece right side out.

4 Press the raw edge of the straight end with the rickrack to the inside. Press the straight end of the wool to the inside as well, keeping the excess wool for stability and easier sewing. Hand stitch the opening closed.

5 Sew one half of the snap to the wool side of the curved end, centered from side to side and measuring ¼" from the edge of the snap to the edge of the project. Position the other half of the snap on the embroidered side of the piece, centering it from side to side and measuring 6½" from the edge of the snap to the straight edge of the project. Sew in place.

6 Fold the project into quarters and snap it closed.

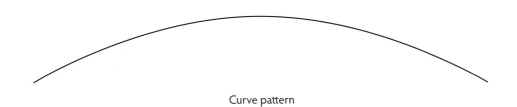

Curve pattern

Embroidery key

- ----- Backstitch
- >>>> Couching
- >>>>> Feather stitch
- ∨ Fly stitch
- • French knot
- – – – Running stitch
- ▨ Satin stitch
- —— Stem stitch
- ⟨⟨⟨⟨ Wheatear stitch

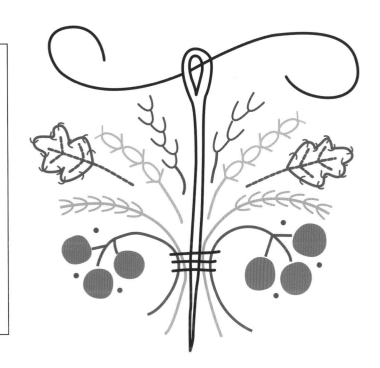

Black Satin Sachet

Black Satin is a variety of blackberry that I love. Stitch these berries on a little sachet where they will warm your heart every time you reach in your closet.

FINISHED SIZE
4" × 6", EXCLUDING RIBBON HANGER

Materials

6" × 8" rectangle of cream print for embroidery background

8" × 10" rectangle of green print for border and backing

4" × 11" rectangle of scrap fabric for interior pouch

6" × 8" rectangle of lightweight batting

12" length of ⅜"-wide black grosgrain ribbon

2 black buttons, ⅝" diameter

½ cup of dried lavender buds for filling

Embroidery Floss

Colors listed below are for The Gentle Art embroidery floss. For DMC equivalents, see page 75.

Piney Woods (medium olive green) for leaves, stems, and thorns

Raven (greenish black) for berries

Cutting

From the green print, cut:

1 rectangle, 4" × 4½"

1 square, 4½" × 4½"

2 rectangles, 1" × 5½"

2 rectangles, 1" × 4½"

From the scrap fabric, cut:

2 rectangles, 3" × 5"

Embroidering the Design

1 Find the center of the cream rectangle by gently finger-pressing the rectangle in half vertically and horizontally.

2 Trace the embroidery pattern on page 21 in the center of the cream rectangle.

3 Referring to "Embroidery Stitches" on page 76, use two strands of floss to embroider the design, following the embroidery key next to the pattern.

4 When the embroidery is complete, press well.

Assembling the Sachet

Sew with a ¼" seam allowance and press the seam allowances as indicated by the arrows.

1 Place the batting on the wrong side of the embroidered piece and quilt as desired. I quilted a diagonal grid in the background with the stitching lines about ¼" apart.

2 Trim the piece to 3½" × 5½".

3 Sew a green 1" × 5½" rectangle to each side of the embroidered piece and press. Sew a green 1" × 4½" rectangle to the top and bottom. Press. The sachet measures 4½" × 6½", including the seam allowances.

4 Turn under ¼" on one of the 4½" sides of each remaining green rectangle and press. Turn under ¼" again and press. Topstitch to create hems for the backing pieces.

5 With right sides together, place the smaller backing rectangle on the embroidery piece, aligning the raw edges. Add the larger backing rectangle with the wrong side up, aligning raw edges and overlapping the first rectangle. Pin in place. Sew all the way around the piece using a ¼" seam allowance. Clip the corners. Turn right side out and press.

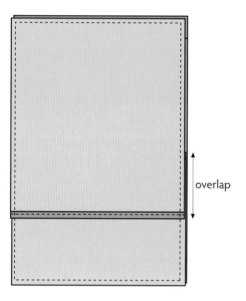

overlap

6 Stitch in the ditch of the border seam—in the background, right next to the seam.

7 Trim the ends of the grosgrain ribbon at a 45° angle and singe the ends with a match to keep them from fraying.

8 Place the ribbon at the top two corners of the sachet so the ends extend 1" below the top border. Sew a button at each corner over the ribbon to secure it in place.

9 With right sides together, sew the two 3" × 5" scrap rectangles together on three sides, leaving one 3" end open. Turn right side out and press.

10 Turn under ¼" on the open end and press. Fill with the lavender and then machine stitch the end closed.

11 Insert the lavender-filled pouch inside the embroidered pouch through the opening in the back to complete the sachet.

Embroidery key

ᴏᴏᴏᴏᴏ Chain stitch

▨ Satin stitch

—— Stem stitch

— Straight stitch

Plentiful Coat Pin

Spice up that warm fall jacket or scarf
with this perky little blackbird pin.

FINISHED SIZE
2" × 3½"

Materials

6" × 8" rectangle of cream print for embroidery background

3" × 5" rectangle of green print for backing and pin sleeve

3" × 5" rectangle of lightweight batting

18" length of ¼"-wide green rickrack (size #17)

1 Dritz skirt/kilt pin, 3"

Embroidery Floss

Colors listed below are for The Gentle Art embroidery floss. For DMC equivalents, see page 75.

Moss (dark olive green) for leaves

Picnic Basket (brown) for branches and stems

Raven (greenish black) for bird and berries

Cutting

From the green print, cut:

1 rectangle, 2½" × 4"

1 rectangle, 1" × 2"

Embroidering the Design

1 Find the center of the cream rectangle by gently finger-pressing the rectangle in half vertically and horizontally.

2 Trace the embroidery pattern on page 24 in the center of the cream rectangle.

3 Referring to "Embroidery Stitches" on page 76, use two strands of floss to embroider the designs, following the embroidery key next to the pattern. For the blackberries, use six strands of floss and three wraps to make the French knots. For the leaves on the berries, stitch a lazy daisy with a straight stitch in the middle.

4 When the embroidery is complete, press well.

Finishing

1 Place the batting on the wrong side of the embroidered piece centered behind the stitching; baste and quilt around the designs as desired. I stitched the piece randomly, adding stitches in the bird body as well as in the background.

2 Trim the quilted embroidery piece to 2½" × 4", keeping the design centered.

3 Starting at the center of the bottom, leave a 1" tail and baste the rickrack onto the right side of the embroidery using a scant ¼" seam allowance, stitching through the center of the rickrack. Overlap the rickrack at the bottom. Cut the end of the rickrack, leaving a 1" tail.

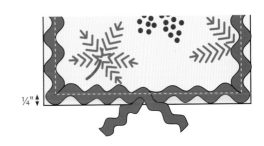

6 Insert the skirt/kilt pin into the hanger sleeve so that the stationary side is encased within the sleeve. Hand stitch the pin sleeve to the back.

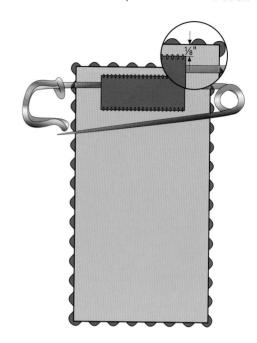

4 Place the green 2½" × 4" rectangle right sides together with the embroidered piece. Sew together using a ¼" seam allowance and leaving the bottom open. Trim the corners and turn the piece right side out. Turn under and press the unsewn edges ¼" to the inside. Slip the rickrack tails to the inside and hand stitch the opening closed.

5 Turn under ¼" on all sides of the green 1" × 2" rectangle and press. Pin in place on the back of the embroidered piece, centered from side to side and ⅛" from the top edge.

Embroidery key

>>>>>> Fishbone stitch

• French knot

◯ Lazy daisy

‒ ‒ ‒ Running stitch

——— Stem stitch

— Straight stitch

Gather Together Runner

Fall is a time for families to gather around the table and be thankful. This table runner will make everyone feel right at home.

FINISHED SIZE
12½" × 28½"

Materials

½ yard of cream print for embroidery background

⅞ yard of green print for backing and binding

18" × 34" rectangle of lightweight batting

Removable fabric marker or quilter's masking tape

Embroidery Floss

Colors listed below are for The Gentle Art embroidery floss. For DMC equivalents, see page 75.

Cidermill Brown (light brown variegated) for Chinese lantern shells

Gingersnap (orange brown) for Chinese lantern berries and acorn nuts

Moss (dark olive green) for medium leaves

Mulberry (dark brown red) for pears, red berries, and pomegranates

Mustard Seed (yellow green) for large leaves

Picnic Basket (brown) for stems and acorn tops

Piney Woods (medium olive green) for large leaves, small leaves, and fig and blackberry leaves

Raven (greenish black) for blackberries

Tin Bucket (blue gray) for figs

Cutting

From the cream print, cut:
1 rectangle, 18" × 34"

From the green print, cut:
1 rectangle, 18" × 34"

3 strips, 2½" × 42"

Embroidering the Design

1 Mark a rectangle that measures 10" × 26" on the cream background using a removable fabric marker or quilter's masking tape, or by lightly pressing creases in the fabric. There should be 4" all around the rectangle.

2 Trace the embroidery pattern on page 27 parallel to one 18" end, keeping the design just inside the marked line. Turn the pattern (or fabric) 90° and trace the pattern twice on each long side and again on the opposite end, as shown.

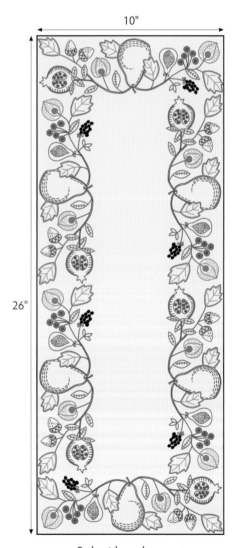

Embroidery placement

Nestle Your Stem Stitches

When you see two lines of stem stitches next to each other in the embroidery pattern, stitch so that the lines touch.

3 Referring to "Embroidery Stitches" on page 76, use two strands of floss to embroider the designs, following the embroidery key next to the pattern.

4 When the embroidery is complete, press well.

Finishing

1 Place the green 18" × 34" backing piece wrong side up on your work surface. Layer the batting and then the embroidered piece on top with the right side up. Baste the layers together.

2 Quilt inside the embroidered design as desired. I quilted a diagonal grid inside the design and outline quilted the embroidered designs.

3 Trim the finished quilted piece to 12½" × 28½", keeping the design centered.

4 Bind the table runner using the green 2½" × 42" strips as you would a quilt.

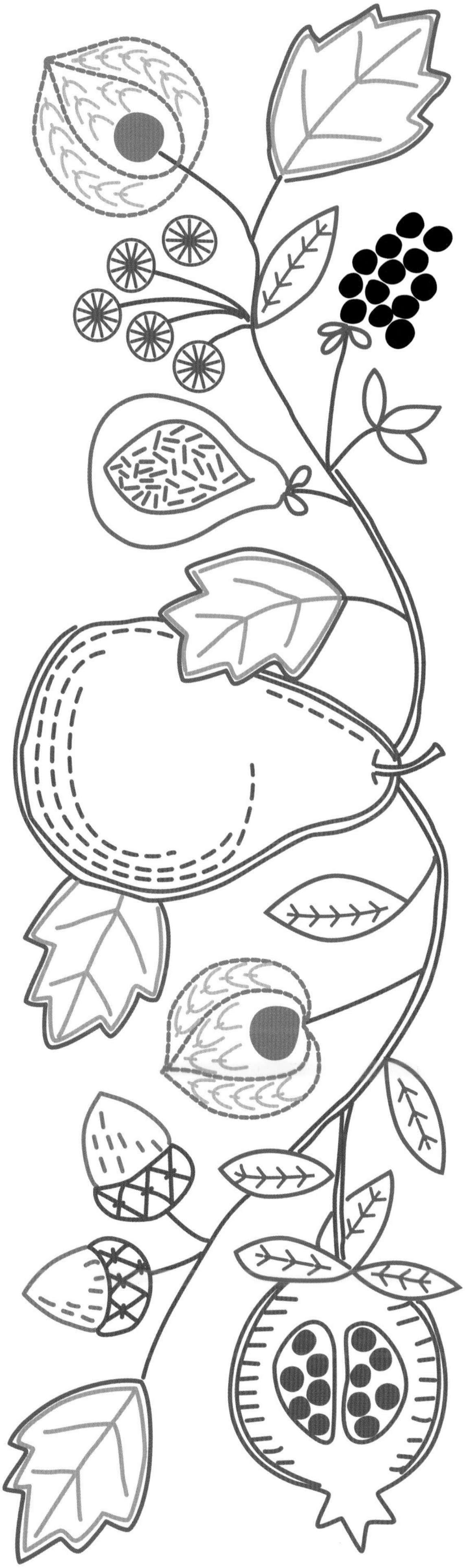

Embroidery key

------ Backstitch	Seed stitch
↠↠↠ Fern sitch	——— Stem stitch
∨ Fly stitch	— Straight stitch
Lazy daisy stitch	✕ Straight stitch with anchor
— — — Running stitch	⊛ Wagon wheel stitch
Satin stitch	

Give Thanks

Greet your visitors with a message of
thanks with this small framed piece.

FINISHED SIZE
8" × 10", EXCLUDING FRAME

Materials

12" × 14" rectangle of cream print for embroidery

12" × 14" rectangle of lightweight batting

11" × 13" wooden frame with 7⅝" × 9⅝" interior opening*

Archival tape for securing the embroidery piece in the frame

Brads for securing the frame backing (optional; see step 3 of "Finishing" on page 30)

If the frame doesn't come with cardboard, you'll need two 8" × 10" pieces of cardboard. The embroidery piece will be wrapped around one piece, and the other will be used as a backing.

Embroidery Floss

Colors listed below are for The Gentle Art embroidery floss. For DMC equivalents, see page 75.

Autumn Leaves (yellow gold) for yellow pods and bird's beak

Burnt Orange (pale orange) for oak leaves

Cidermill Brown (light brown variegated) for large acorn cap

Country Redwood (wine red) for red pods

Gingersnap (orange brown) for large and small acorns

Picnic Basket (brown) for brown stems, small acorn caps, large acorn-cap interior, and woven fill

Piney Woods (medium olive green) for green stems, banner, and yellow pod accents

Raven (greenish black) for lettering

Tin Bucket (blue gray) for bird, blueberries, and blue dots

Embroidering the Design

1 Find the center of the cream rectangle by gently finger-pressing the rectangle in half vertically and horizontally.

2 Using the embroidery pattern on page 31, trace the design onto the cream rectangle.

3 Referring to "Embroidery Stitches" on page 76, use two strands of floss to embroider the designs, following the embroidery key next to the pattern.

4 When the embroidery is complete, press well.

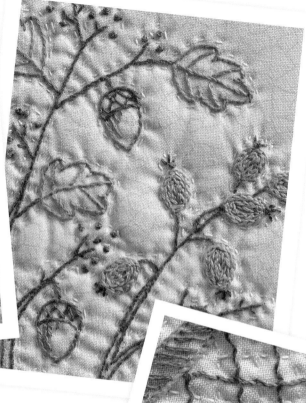

Finishing

1 Place the batting on the wrong side of the embroidered piece. Add quilting stitches as desired. I quilted an outline around the stitching.

2 Center the piece on the 8" × 10" backing board that came with the frame. Fold the edges of the fabric over the cardboard, making sure the fabric is taut but not distorted. Secure the fabric and batting with archival tape.

3 Cover the back of the project with a second piece of cardboard. Insert the embroidery piece into the frame and secure with small brads or use the clips that came with the frame.

Reduce Bulk

I trimmed the batting to 8" × 10" after quilting to reduce bulk when framing.

Embroidery key

- - - - - - Backstitch

∞∞∞∞ Chain stitch

∨ Fly stitch

• French knot

– – – Running stitch

—— Stem stitch

— Straight stitch

⊛ Wagon wheel stitch

〜 Whipped running stitch

3 wraps

3 wraps

1 wrap

in all things
Give Thanks

Great Rewards Kitchen Towels

Cherries, acorns, and a carrot offer delicious rewards to these woodland friends.

FINISHED SIZE
17" × 27"

Materials for 3 Towels

3 kitchen towels*

*I used kitchen towels made by Dunroven House; see "Resources" on page 79.

Embroidery Floss

Colors listed below are for The Gentle Art embroidery floss. For DMC equivalents, see page 75.

Cinnamon (reddish brown) for all

Raven (greenish black) for all

Embroidering the Design

1 Using the embroidery patterns on pages 34 and 35, trace a different design onto each kitchen towel, placing the utensil handles 5" up from the bottom edge and centering the designs from side to side.

2 Referring to "Embroidery Stitches" on page 76, use two strands of floss, one of each color, to embroider the designs, following the embroidery key next to the pattern.

Embroidery key

ᴠ Fly stitch

- - - Running stitch

——— Stem stitch

— Straight stitch

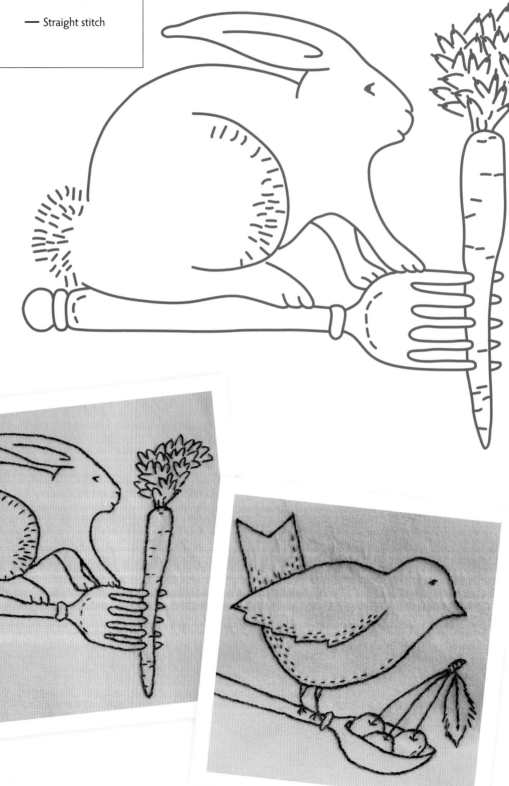

Embroidery key

- - - - Running stitch

———— Stem stitch

— Straight stitch

✗ Straight stitch
  with anchor

Embroidery key

• French knot

- - - - Running stitch

———— Stem stitch

— Straight stitch

Harvest Pillow

*Cozy up with a pillow adorned in oak leaves and acorns—
the perfect accompaniment when enjoying a fall fire.*

FINISHED SIZE
18½" × 18½"

Materials

¾ yard of cream tone on tone for embroidery
background and pillow back

22" × 22" square of lightweight batting

18" × 18" pillow form

Embroidery Floss

*Colors listed below are for The Gentle Art embroidery
floss. For DMC equivalents, see page 75.*

Country Redwood (wine red) for leaves, berries,
and branch ties

Moss (dark olive green) for dots and acorn nuts

Picnic Basket (brown) for branches, stems, and
acorn caps

Cutting

From the cream tone on tone, cut:

1 square, 22" × 22"

2 rectangles, 12" × 19"

Embroidering the Design

1 Find the center of the cream square by gently finger-pressing the square in half vertically and horizontally.

2 Aligning the center crosshairs on the embroidery pattern on page 39 with the center of the fabric, trace the corner embroidery pattern four times, rotating it as shown to complete the design.

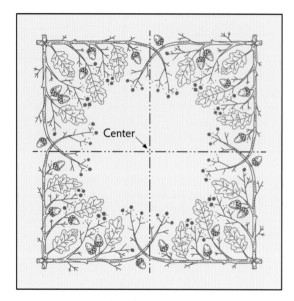

Center

Embroidery placement

3 Referring to "Embroidery Stitches" on page 76, use two strands of floss to embroider the designs, following the embroidery key next to the pattern.

4 When the embroidery is complete, press well.

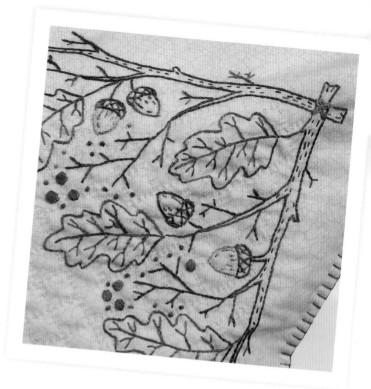

Assembling the Pillow

1 Place the batting square on the wrong side of the embroidery piece and baste the layers together. Quilt as desired. I quilted a diagonal grid in the center of the design, with stitching lines ½" apart.

2 When the quilting is complete, trim the finished pillow top to 19" square, keeping the design centered.

3 To make the pillow back, turn under ½" on one 12" edge of a cream rectangle and press. Turn under ½" again, press, and topstitch. Repeat with the other cream rectangle.

4 With right sides together, pin the front to the backing pieces, overlapping the hemmed edges of the two backing pieces and having raw edges aligned. Sew around the outer edges using a ¼" seam allowance.

5 Clip the corners and turn the pillow right side out. Press.

6 Using two strands of Country Redwood floss, sew a blanket stitch all the way around the outer edge of the pillow. The stitches should be about ¼" long, the same as the width of the seam allowance.

7 Insert the pillow form through the opening.

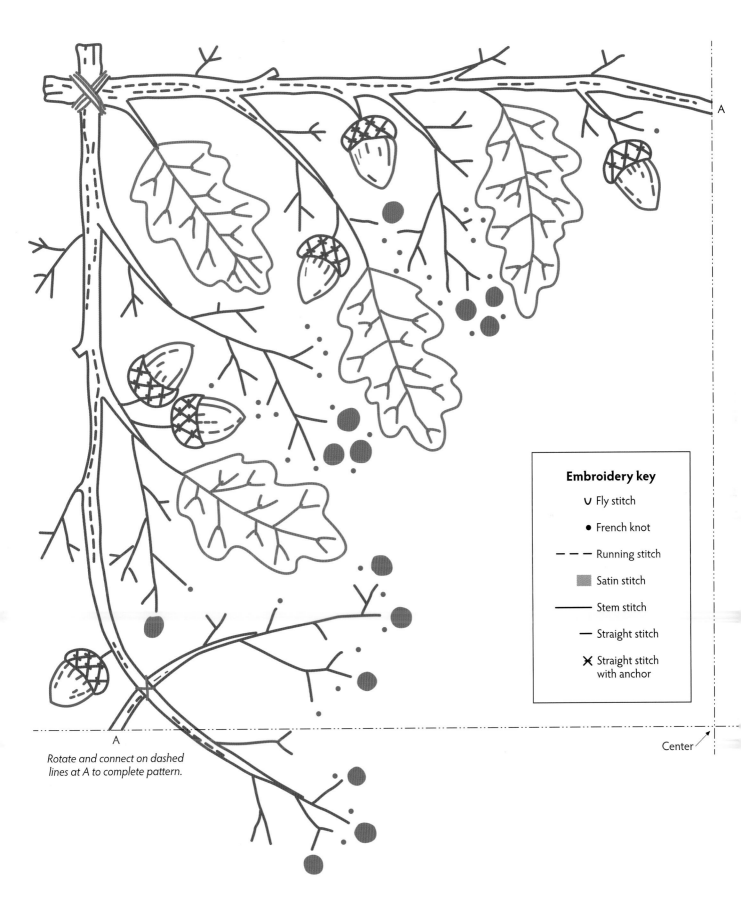

A

Embroidery key

ᴜ Fly stitch

● French knot

– – – Running stitch

▨ Satin stitch

—— Stem stitch

— Straight stitch

✖ Straight stitch with anchor

A

Rotate and connect on dashed lines at A to complete pattern.

Center

Hazel

A sweet woodland rabbit is right at home in the brambles of fall.

FINISHED SIZE
12½" × 15", EXCLUDING HANGER

Materials

16" × 18" rectangle of cream tone on tone for embroidery background

½ yard of gold print for border and backing

16" × 19" rectangle of lightweight batting

Ackfeld wire table stand* (optional)

*See "Resources" on page 79.

Embroidery Floss

Colors listed below are for The Gentle Art embroidery floss. For DMC equivalents, see page 75.

Burnt Orange (pale orange) for orange pods, orange leaves, dots, and rabbit's ears, eyes, and nose

Cidermill Brown (light brown variegated) for rabbit

Cinnamon (reddish brown) for acorn nut

Grape Arbor (dark plum) for blackberries and round berries

Moss (dark olive green) for green leaves

Old Hickory (brown gold) for wheat stalks

Picnic Basket (brown) for branches, brown stems, acorn cap, and rabbit's eyelids

Piney Woods (medium olive green) for green stems and leaves

Cutting

From the gold print, cut:

2 rectangles, 2" × 13"

2 rectangles, 2" × 12½"

2 rectangles, 8" × 13"

1 rectangle, 3" × 11½"

Embroidering the Design

1 Find the center of the cream rectangle by gently finger-pressing the rectangle in half vertically and horizontally.

2 Align the two halves of the embroidery pattern on pages 43 and 44, and trace the design onto the center of the cream rectangle.

3 Referring to "Embroidery Stitches" on page 76, use two strands of floss to embroider the design, following the embroidery key next to the pattern. Use the pink sections of the Burnt Orange thread for the rabbit's ears, eyes, and nose to give them a rosy appearance.

4 When the embroidery is complete, press well.

Assembling the Quilt

Sew with a ¼" seam allowance and press the seam allowances as indicated by the arrows.

1 Trim the embroidery piece to 10" × 12½", keeping the design centered.

2 Sew the gold 2" × 12½" rectangles to the sides of the embroidery and press. Sew the gold print 2" × 13" rectangles to the top and bottom of the embroidery piece and press. The quilt top should measure 13" × 15½".

3 Place the batting on the wrong side of the embroidery and quilt as desired. I quilted an echo around the designs and then filled in the spaces randomly.

4 Using three strands of Moss floss, make a chain stitch along the seamline of the border and embroidery piece. Make another line of chain stitches ½" from the outside edge of the border.

5 Trim the batting even with the embroidered top.

6 Sew the two 8" × 13" backing rectangles together along the 13" sides. Switch to a basting stitch for about 4" in the middle of this seam. Press the seam allowances to one side.

7 With right sides together, pin the embroidery piece to the backing piece. Sew around all four sides. Clip the corners. Remove the basting stitches from the backing seam and turn the piece right side out through this opening. Press. Hand stitch the opening closed.

8 To make a hanging sleeve, turn under ½" on all four sides of the gold 3" × 11½" rectangle and press. Hand stitch it to the wrong side of the finished project, leaving the short ends open and centering the sleeve from side to side and 1" from the top.

9 Insert the wire frame into the sleeve.

Embroidery key	
- - - - - - Backstitch	▨ Satin stitch
⟩⟩⟩⟩ Fern sitch	—— Stem stitch
∨ Fly stitch	— Straight stitch
● French knot	✖ Straight stitch with anchor
◯ Lazy daisy stitch	⟨⟨⟨⟨ Wheatear stitch
– – – Running stitch	

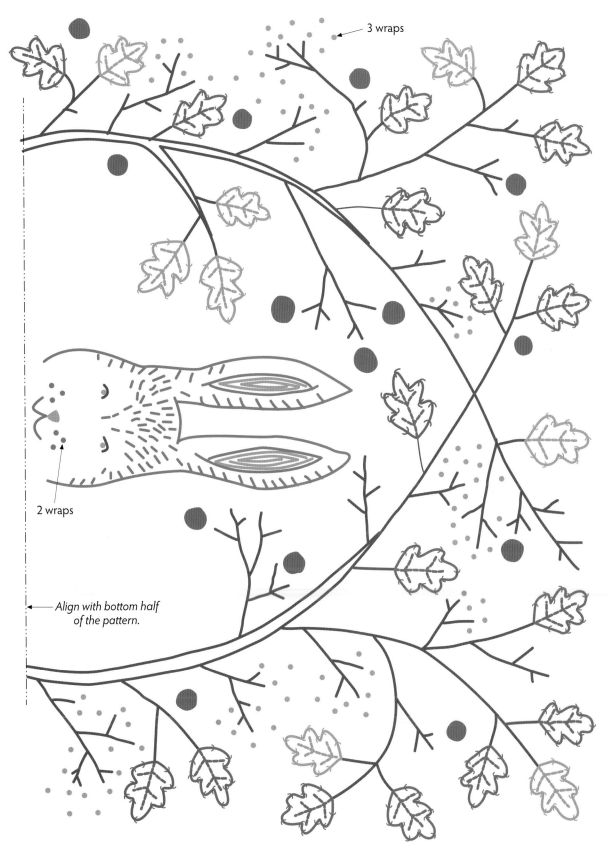

3 wraps

2 wraps

*Align with bottom half
of the pattern.*

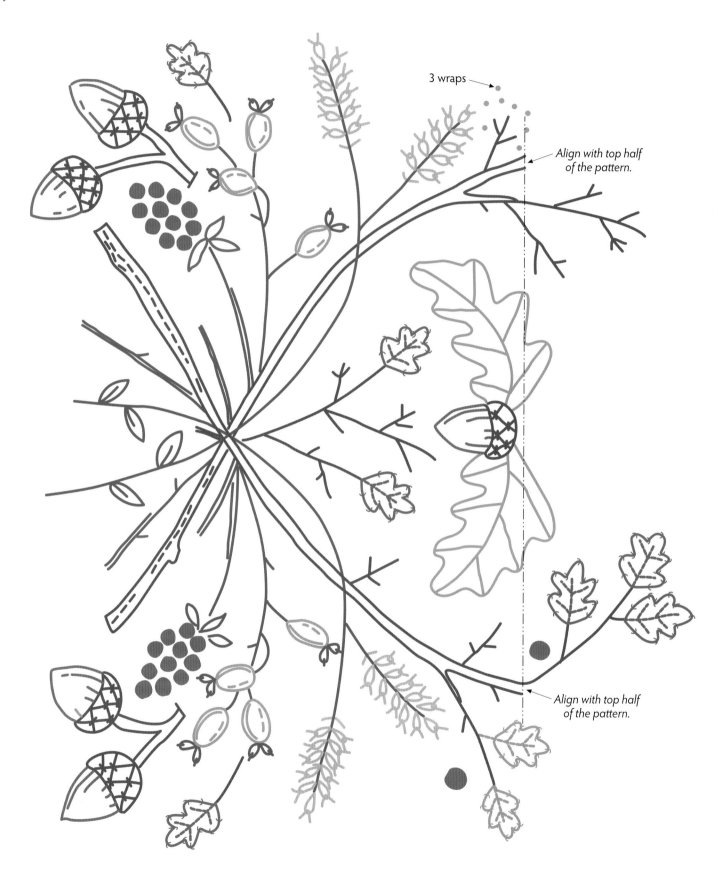

3 wraps

Align with top half of the pattern.

Align with top half of the pattern.

In a Nutshell Purse

*This small purse has a fold-over opening and
is just the right size for those small essentials.*

FINISHED SIZE
8" × 8" WITH FLAP FOLDED;
8" × 11" WITH FLAP OPEN

fold over bag 8"x8"

fill in with chain stitches

Embroidery Floss

Colors listed below are for The Gentle Art embroidery floss. For DMC equivalents, see page 75.

Cinnamon (reddish brown) for acorn nuts

Moss (dark olive green) for leaves and acorn caps

Picnic Basket (brown) for branch and stems

Cutting

From the green stripe, cut:

1 rectangle, 8½" × 22½"

1 rectangle, 3" × 8½"

1 rectangle, 1" × 8½"

1 strip, 3" × 20"

From the brown solid, cut:

1 rectangle, 8½" × 11½"

1 square, 8½" × 8½"

1 rectangle, 6" × 8½"

2 strips, 3" × 42"

Materials

6" × 10" rectangle of cream tone on tone for embroidery background

⅓ yard of green stripe for accent and lining

½ yard of brown solid for purse body*

6" × 10" piece of lightweight batting

Fabric marker, pencil, or permanent pen

I used a canvas-weight cotton for the purse shown.

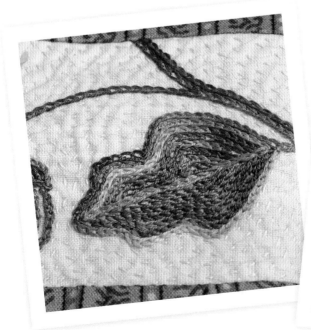

Embroidering the Design

1 Trace the embroidery pattern on page 49 onto the center of the cream rectangle. Because all of the stitching is a chain stitch, it's only necessary to trace the outlines of the leaves and acorns and a line for the stems. The rectangle on the pattern indicates the cutting lines after the embroidery is complete. Mark the rectangle with a pencil or fabric marker that will not disappear when ironed.

2 Referring to "Embroidery Stitches" on page 76, use two strands of floss to embroider the designs using a chain stitch. Stitch the outlines of the leaves and acorns first, and then fill in with chain stitches.

3 When the embroidery is complete, press well. Place the batting on the wrong side of the embroidery piece. Quilt as desired. I quilted closely spaced lines that echo the shapes in the design. Press again if needed. Trim to 3" × 8½" following the marked guidelines.

Assembling the Purse

Sew with a ¼" seam allowance and press the seam allowances as indicated by the arrows.

1 Sew the green 1" × 8½" rectangle to what will be the top of the embroidered piece. Press. Sew the brown 8½" square to the green rectangle and press.

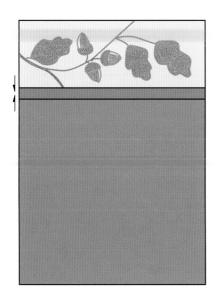

2 Fold the green 3" × 8½" rectangle in half lengthwise, with wrong sides together, and press. Sew the raw edges of the folded rectangle to the 8½" edge of the brown 6" × 8½" rectangle for the pocket, right sides together. Press and fold over to the wrong side to create a binding. Hand stitch the folded edge of the accent fabric to the wrong side of the brown pocket rectangle.

3 To make the straps, fold a brown 3" × 42" strip in half lengthwise with right sides together. Sew the long raw edges together to form a tube. Repeat with the second brown 3" × 42" strip. Turn the tubes right side out and press so the seam allowance is along the side of the strap.

4 Place the embroidered section right side up on a work surface. Place the two strap ends so that they're even with the bottom, 1" in from the sides, and the seam of the strap is toward the inside of the purse. Pin in place. Stitch the straps close to the edges, sewing along the bottom, up 6", across, and back down again to create a stitched rectangle.

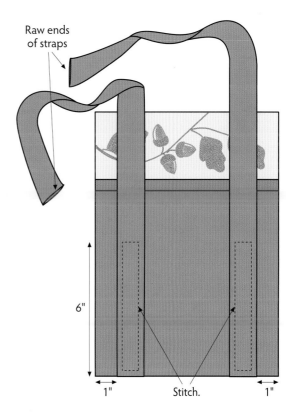

Raw ends of straps

6"

1"   Stitch.   1"

5 Place the pocket piece from step 2 right side up on top of the stitched handle straps, with the green accent strip along the top, toward the embroidered end.

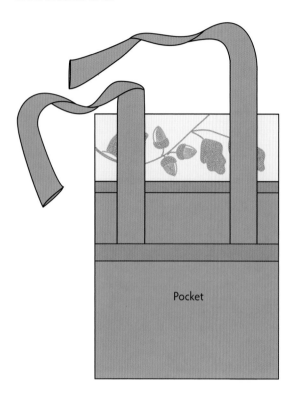

Pocket

6 Place the brown 8½" × 11½" rectangle wrong side up on top of the pocket and embroidered piece with straps, aligning the raw edges. Pin along the sides, making sure the only place the straps are caught is in the seam at the bottom of the bag. Sew down one side, across the bottom of the bag, and up the other side, being careful not to catch the straps in the side seam.

7 Clip the corners and turn the bag right side out. Press.

Adding the Lining

Sew all seams with a ¼" seam allowance.

1 Fold the green 8½" × 22½" lining rectangle in half, with right sides together, to form a rectangle that is 8½" × 11¼". Sew both 11¼" sides of the lining. *Do not turn right side out.*

2 Slip the lining inside the bag, aligning the top raw edges and matching the side seams. Baste around the top of the bag a scant ¼" from the raw edges.

3 Fold the green 3" × 20" strip in half lengthwise with wrong sides together. Cut the starting end at a 45° angle in the direction shown.

4 Leaving a 2" tail at the angled end of the accent binding and starting at the center back of the bag, pin the raw edges of the binding to the raw edges of the bag top on the outside. Starting at the 2" mark, sew the binding to the bag top, stopping 4" from where you started sewing.

5 Open the end of the folded binding strip and trim at a 45° angle (the same direction as the starting end) so that it overlaps the beginning of the binding by 2". Turn under ¼" on the raw edge of the angled cut and press.

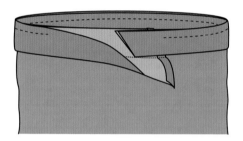

6 Slip the starting end of the binding inside the open end, and then fold it in half again. Adjust the overlap so that it fits the length needed to complete the binding of the bag top. Finish sewing the binding in place. Fold it over to the inside of the bag and hand stitch in place.

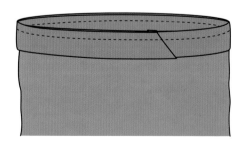

Finishing the Handles

1 To adjust the handle strap to your desired length, pin the ends of the handle straps together so the purse hangs where you like it and the seam will be at your shoulder. Mark this place on the straps.

2 Cut both strap ends ½" *beyond* the marked point. Fold one end ½" to the inside and press. Slip the other strap end ½" inside the folded one. Sew across the end to secure the ends together without any raw edges showing.

3 Sew the handles in place 1" above the pocket by machine or by hand, as shown. To machine sew the handles, open the top of the purse and manipulate the layers so that you sew through the outer purse fabric and lining only.

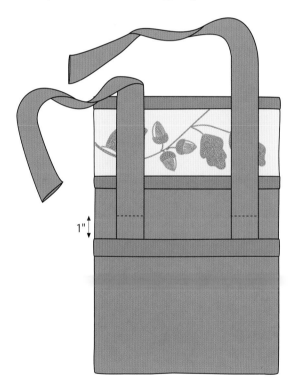

1"

4 Fill the bag with your essentials and fold the embroidered flap over.

Top

Leave unstitched to make a "highlight."

Embroidery key

∞∞∞∞ Chain stitch

Nutty's Nest Notion Keeper

Pockets, pockets, pockets! There's room to squirrel away lots of sewing notions in this little folded notion keep.

FINISHED SIZE
5" × 5½" CLOSED; 5½" × 14½" OPEN

Materials

1 fat quarter (18" × 21") of cream tone on tone for embroidery background and pocket accents

¼ yard of brown print for pockets

8" × 18" rectangle of lightweight batting

1 button, ⅝" diameter

Cord maker* (optional)

See "Resources" on page 79. As an alternative to making cording, you can use 1½ yards of chenille yarn or other trim.

Embroidery Floss

Colors listed below are for The Gentle Art embroidery floss, except where noted for the accent cording and tie. For DMC equivalents, see page 75.

Brown (DMC 801) for accent cording and tie

Cidermill Brown (light brown variegated) for squirrel

Moss (dark olive green) for leaves, squirrel's sweater and hat, and acorn nuts

Picnic Basket (brown) for stems, acorn caps, and stitching

Raven (greenish black) for needle

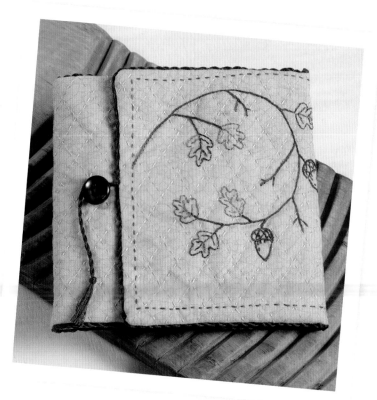

Cutting

From the cream tone on tone, cut:

1 rectangle, 8" × 18"

3 rectangles, 3" × 6"

From the brown print, cut:

1 strip, 6" × 42"

Embroidering the Design

1 Trace the embroidery patterns on page 55 onto the cream 8" × 18" rectangle as shown, centering the squirrel design from top to bottom. Trace the acorn 3½" away from the point of the needle.

2 Referring to "Embroidery Stitches" on page 76, use two strands of floss to embroider the designs, following the embroidery key next to the pattern.

3 When the embroidery is complete, press well.

Quilting the Design

1 Place the batting on the wrong side of the embroidered piece. Quilt as desired. I quilted a diagonal grid around the squirrel and random stitches inside the squirrel.

2 Trim the embroidered and quilted piece to 6" × 15"; the cutting line should be ½" outside the brown running stitches.

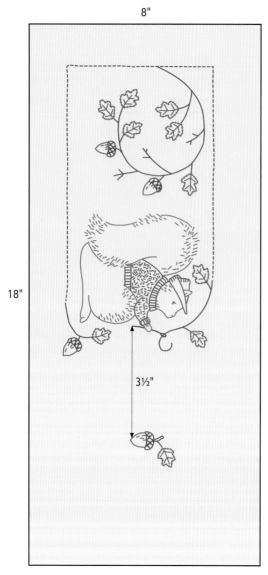

Embroidery placement

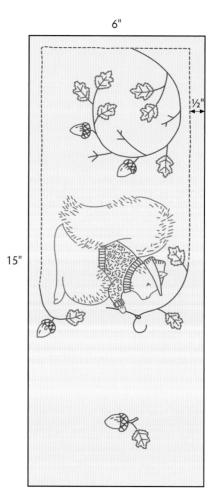

Making the Pockets

1 To create the pockets, begin at the right end of the brown 6" × 42" strip and mark in increments measuring 5", 4", 8½", 5", 8½", and 4". Fold it in an accordion manner as shown to create the pockets. Press well and pin the three folds that will become the pocket tops. Trim the piece along the pocket bottom end so that the folded length measures 15".

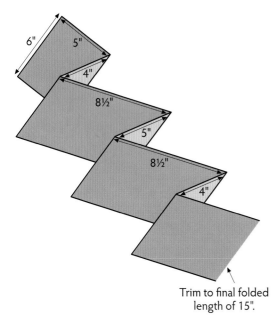

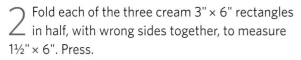

Trim to final folded length of 15".

2 Fold each of the three cream 3" × 6" rectangles in half, with wrong sides together, to measure 1½" × 6". Press.

3 Using a ¼" seam allowance, sew the raw edges of a cream strip to each pocket fold as you would with a quilt binding. Press upward and fold over to the other side so that the folded edge aligns with the stitching on the other side. Hand stitch the cream strips in place.

4 Using two strands of Picnic Basket brown floss, sew a blanket stitch along the top edge of each cream strip and a running stitch ⅛" from the bottom edge.

5 Refold and pin the pockets in place. Baste along the two long sides using a scant ¼" seam allowance.

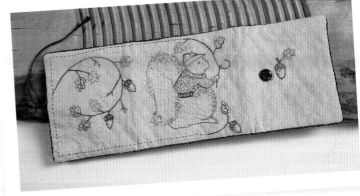

Assembling the Notion Keeper

1 Place the pocket section right sides together with the embroidered section. The pocket opening should be at the end with the single embroidered acorn. Sew together the sides and the end with the pocket opening using a ¼" seam allowance. Leave the end at the pocket bottom unsewn.

2 Clip the corners and trim any bulky seams. Turn the piece right side out and press. Turn the bottom edges ¼" to the inside and press. Hand stitch the opening closed.

3 For the cording, cut a 240" length of Brown DMC floss. Referring to "Cord Making" on page 78, make 48" of cording. This is a *really* long length of thread, and it may require an extra set of hands.

4 Starting from the center of the short edge with the brown running stitches and the folded end of the cording, whipstitch along the seamline. Use one strand of the Brown floss so that it will match the cording. When the cording comes around and meets where it began, add a few security stitches to add extra strength. Measure 6" of the "tail" of the cording and tie a knot. Cut off the excess cording past the knot.

5 Sew the button to the exterior of the keeper, centered side to side and 3" in from the short edge as shown above. To close and secure the notion holder, fold into thirds and wrap the tail of the cording around the button.

Embroidery key

- ➤➤➤➤ Couching
- ⬭ Lazy daisy stitch
- – – – Running stitch
- 🖌 Seed stitch
- —— Stem stitch
- — Straight stitch
- ✕ Straight stitch with anchor

Use 1 strand of floss for needle.

Wild Oaks Pincushion

*Even pins enjoy a pretty home. This large pincushion
will stay securely on the arm of your favorite chair.*

FINISHED SIZE
8" × 5"

Materials

8" × 10" rectangle of cream tone on tone for embroidery background

5½" × 8½" rectangle of coordinating or contrasting print for backing

8" × 10" rectangle of lightweight batting

2 cups of ground walnut shells for filling

Cord maker* (optional)

See "Resources" on page 79. As an alternative to making cording, you can purchase 1 yard of chenille yarn or other trim.

Embroidery Floss

Colors listed below are for The Gentle Art embroidery floss. For DMC equivalents, see page 75.

Green Tea Leaf (muted green) for letters

Piney Woods (medium olive green) for leaves and border

Pomegranate (dark pink) for dots and border

DMC floss in a color to coordinate with the embroidery and backing fabric for cording

Embroidering the Design

1 Find the center of the cream rectangle by gently finger-pressing the rectangle in half vertically and horizontally.

2 Trace the embroidery pattern on page 59 in the center of the cream rectangle.

3 Referring to "Embroidery Stitches" on page 76, use two strands of floss, unless otherwise indicated, to embroider the designs following the embroidery key next to the pattern.

4 When the embroidery is complete, press well.

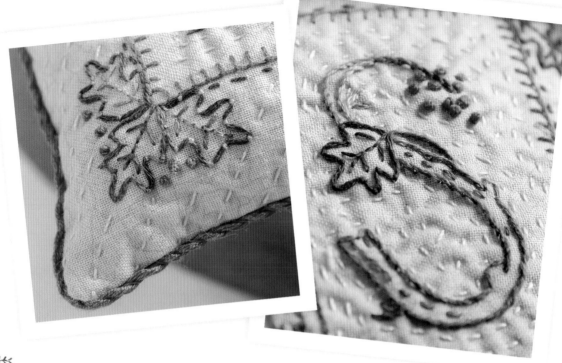

Friendship is a sheltering tree

Assembling the Pincushion

1 Place the batting on the wrong side of the embroidered piece and quilt as desired. I echo quilted around the letters in the center and quilted diagonal lines in the border area.

2 Trim the quilted piece to 5½" × 8½", keeping the design centered.

3 With right sides together, sew the embroidered piece to the backing rectangle using a ¼" seam allowance. Leave a 2" opening at the center of the bottom edge for turning. Clip the corners and turn right side out.

4 For the cording, cut a 140" length of the DMC floss. Referring to "Cord Making" on page 78, make 28" of cording using all six strands of the floss.

5 Use one strand of matching floss to whipstitch the cording around the edge of the pincushion, starting at the middle of the opening. Leave a 1" tail of cording at the beginning and at the end.

Opening

6 Fill the pincushion with the ground walnut shells. Hand stitch the opening closed, making sure the cording tails are hidden securely inside of the pincushion.

Embroidery key

- ------ Backstitch
- ⊔⊔⊔⊔ Blanket stitch
- ⟩⟩⟩⟩ Couching
- ● French knot (3 wraps)
- – – Running stitch
- —— Stem stitch

Welcome Home

All paths lead home. This welcoming path leads to a comfy cottage through a cornucopia of splendid fall colors.

FINISHED SIZE
12" × 9", EXCLUDING HANGER

Materials

12" × 16" rectangle of cream tone on tone for embroidery background

¼ yard (or 1 fat quarter) of green tone on tone for border and backing

12" × 16" rectangle of lightweight batting

Ackfeld wire 12" dowel hanger*

*See "Resources" on page 79.

Embroidery Floss

Colors listed below are for The Gentle Art embroidery floss. For DMC equivalents, see page 75.

Cidermill Brown (light brown variegated) for trees and fence

Gingersnap (orange brown) for pumpkin, acorns, and cornucopia

Moss (dark olive green) for green berries, wheat stalks, pathway, and hill

Old Hickory (brown gold) for oak leaves and dots

Picnic Basket (brown) for branches, stems, and acorn caps

Piney Woods (medium olive green) for green oak leaves

Ruby Slipper (rosy red) for red oak leaves, red berries, roof, and door

Tin Bucket (blue gray) for birds and gray parts of house

Cutting

From the green tone on tone, cut:

2 rectangles, 6½" × 9½"

1 rectangle, 2½" × 12"

2 strips, 1" × 11½"

2 strips, 1" × 9½"

Embroidering the Design

1 Find the center of the cream rectangle by gently finger-pressing the rectangle in half vertically and horizontally.

2 Trace the embroidery pattern on page 63 in the center of the cream rectangle.

3 Referring to "Embroidery Stitches" on page 76, use two strands of floss to embroider the designs, following the embroidery key next to the pattern.

4 When the embroidery is complete, press well.

Finishing

Sew with a ¼" seam allowance and press the seam allowances as indicated by the arrows.

1 Trim the embroidered piece to measure 8½" × 11½", keeping the design centered.

2 Sew the green 1" × 11½" strips to the top and bottom of the embroidered piece and press. Sew the green 1" × 9½" strips to the sides and press. The project should measure 9½" × 12½", including the seam allowances.

3 Place the batting on the wrong side of the embroidered piece. Quilt as desired. I quilted echoing lines inside the design and quilted around the stitching. Trim the batting even with the embroidered top.

4 With right sides together, join the two 6½" × 9½" rectangles along the 9½" side. Switch to a basting stitch for about 4" in the middle of this seam. Press the seam allowances to one side.

5 Place the pieced backing and the embroidery right sides together. Pin in place. Sew around all four sides. Clip the corners. Remove the basting stitches from the backing seam, turn the project right side out, and hand stitch the opening closed. Press well.

6 Stitch in the ditch around the border (sew on the cream fabric, right next to the seam).

7 To make the hanging sleeve, turn under the edges of the green 2½" × 12" rectangle ¼" all around and press. Place the sleeve on the back of the project, centered from side to side and ½" from the top. Pin in place and hand stitch. Insert the dowel of the wire hanger into the hanging sleeve.

Embroidery key

------ Backstitch

⋙ Couching

ᴠ Fly stitch

● French knot (3 wraps)

– – – Running stitch

▮ Satin stitch

— Stem stitch

– Straight stitch

✗ Straight stitch with anchor

⋘⋙ Wheatear stitch

Crimson Bounty Tote

Bring this large sling tote to the farmers' market and fill it to your heart's content with autumn fruit such as apples, pears, and persimmons.

FINISHED SIZE
15" × 12" × 2", EXCLUDING HANDLE

Materials

3 yards of 16"-wide toweling for tote and handle*

Transfer-Eze (optional)

This yardage is enough to make the three Nature's Finest Pouches on page 69 from leftover fabric. If you want to make just the tote bag, 2¼ yards is enough if you piece the handle. For a one-piece handle without seams, you'll still need 3 yards. The fabric used in the sample is Flag Day Farm toweling by Moda.

Thread

I used Valdani pearl cotton in color P1. You can use any red 12-weight pearl cotton. Or substitute red embroidery floss and stitch with two strands.

Cutting

See the cutting guide below. You do not need to cut off any selvages; they will keep the fabric from fraying.

From the toweling, cut:

1 rectangle, 16" × 28"

From the remaining toweling, cut:

1 strip, 4½" × 80"*

1 rectangle, 8" × 9"

If you're piecing the handle, cut 2 strips, 4½" × 41", centering them on the stripes.

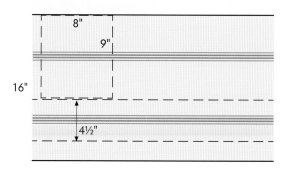

Cutting guide for pocket and handle

Embroidering the Design

1 Zigzag stitch along the cut raw edges of the toweling rectangles to prevent raveling.

2 Trace the embroidery pattern on page 68 onto the 16" × 28" toweling rectangle, centering it between the red stripes and placing the oak leaf 3" from the top edge of the toweling as shown. See "Make Tracing Easy" at right.

Trace the embroidery pattern on page 68

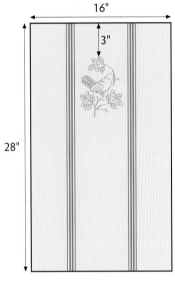

Embroidery placement

3 Referring to "Embroidery Stitches" on page 76, use one strand of pearl cotton (or two strands of embroidery floss) to embroider all of the designs using a backstitch. Stitch a French knot for the bird's eye.

4 When the embroidery is complete, press well.

Make Tracing Easy

The toweling is fairly thick. It *is* possible to see through it to trace the design, but you might want to try a product such as Transfer-Eze. You can photocopy the pattern onto the sew-through, water-soluble product and adhere it to your fabric so that you won't need to trace the design.

Assembling the Bag

1 Turn under ¼" on all four sides of the 8" × 9" rectangle for the pocket and press well. Turn under ¼" again on the 8" sides and on one of the 9" sides and press. On the remaining 9" side, turn under an additional 1" and press.

2 Topstitch along the edge of the 1" hem and along the ¼" hems as well.

3 Pin the pocket piece in place on the wrong side of the bag, centered from side to side. The 1" hem should be 2½" from the end opposite the embroidery.

Wrong side of bag

Pocket placement

4 Sew the pocket in place, stitching one side, across the bottom, and then the other side, sewing close to the folded edges.

5 With right sides together, fold the body of the bag in half. Pin the sides together. Using a ⅝" seam allowance, sew the side seams.

6 Finger-press across the bottom of the bag to make a crease. Bring the side seam and the crease together at the bottom corner of the bag. Measure 1" from the point and draw a line perpendicular to the side seam. Sew along this line. Repeat on the other corner to make gussets.

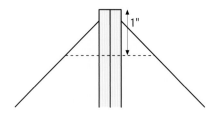

7 Turn the bag right side out and press.

8 Turn under the top of the bag ¼" and press. Fold the top edge under another ½" and press. Topstitch the hem.

Adding the Handle

1 Fold the 4½" × 80" handle strip in half lengthwise with right sides together. Sew the 80" edges together using a ¼" seam allowance and a shorter-than-normal stitch length to create a tube. Turn the tube right side out and press it so that the seam runs along the center. (If you're piecing the handle, sew the two 4½" × 41" strips together first using a ½" seam allowance; press the seam allowances open.)

2 On one end of the handle, turn under 1". Insert the raw end of the handle into the folded end. Sew across the intersection twice to secure the handle into one long continuous loop. Make sure it isn't twisted.

Customize the Handle

You might want to do a trial run with the handle after step 1 to see if the length is satisfactory. You can make it shorter to suit your needs. Cut it to the desired length before sewing the ends in place.

3 Pin the short seam of the handle to the center of the inside bottom of the bag, with the long seam facing up. Pin the handle across the inside bottom of the bag and continue pinning up the side seams. Sew it in place, stitching close to the edge of the handle. This is a little awkward when sewing by machine; pin well and remove the pins as you sew.

Embroidery key

------ Backstitch

● French knot
(3 wraps)

Nature's Finest Pouches

To stay organized, small zippered pouches are
a must. Why not make them pretty too?

FINISHED SIZE
10" × 8"

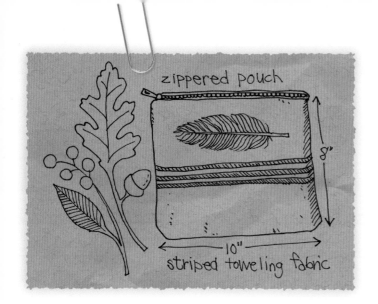

Cutting

See the cutting guide below if you're cutting from toweling yardage. If you're cutting from toweling left over from the tote bag, cut the pieces as wide as your leftover fabric and 11" long. You may not have quite 9½", and that's OK. Just cut the lining rectangles to match. You do not need to cut the selvage edges from the toweling rectangles.

From the toweling, cut:

2 rectangles, 9½" × 11"

From the lining fabric, cut:

2 rectangles, 9½" × 11"

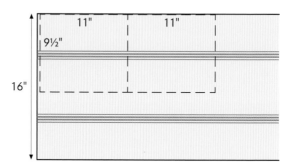

Cutting guide

Materials for 1 Pouch

⅔ yard of 16"-wide toweling with red stripe for pouch*

⅓ yard of fabric for lining

1 nylon zipper, 12" long

Transfer-Eze (optional)

*Or use leftover toweling from Crimson Bounty Tote on page 64. The leftover fabric will be enough to make three pouches. The fabric used in the sample is Flag Day Farm toweling by Moda.

Thread

I used Valdani pearl cotton in color P1. You can use any red 12-weight pearl cotton. Or substitute red embroidery floss and stitch with two strands.

Try Transfer-Eze

The toweling is fairly thick. It *is* possible to see through it to trace the design, but you might want to try a product such as Transfer-Eze. You can photocopy the pattern onto the sew-through, water-soluble product and adhere it to your fabric so that you won't need to trace the design directly onto the fabric.

Embroidering the Designs

1 Zigzag stitch along the raw edges of the toweling rectangles to prevent fraying.

2 Trace the chosen embroidery pattern on page 73 onto one toweling rectangle, centering the design from side to side and placing it ½" or ¾" above the stripe as shown.

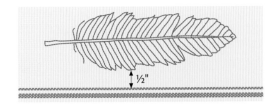

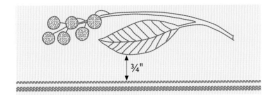

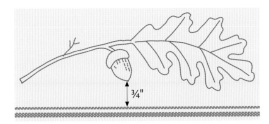

Embroidery placement

3 Referring to "Embroidery Stitches" on page 76, use one strand of pearl cotton (or two strands of floss) to embroider the designs, following the embroidery key next to the pattern. All designs are stitched with backstitches with the exception of the berries, which are filled in using multiple overlapping seed stitches.

4 Once the stitching is complete, press well.

Assembling the Pouch

1 Place the embroidered piece right side up and place the zipper right side down along the top, aligning the edges. The zipper pull should extend past the right end of the toweling; the other end of the zipper should extend at least ¼" past the toweling. Place one lining rectangle on top, right side down, aligning it with the edge of the zipper and embroidered piece. Pin and sew together using a zipper foot, stitching next to the zipper teeth.

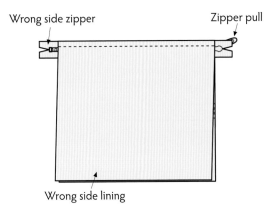

Wrong side zipper   Zipper pull

Wrong side lining

2 Flip the fabric pieces over so the wrong sides are together and press along the sewn edge.

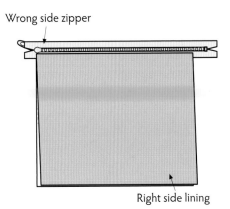

Wrong side zipper

Right side lining

3 Place the second toweling rectangle on the work surface right side up. Place the sewn piece from step 2 on top with the lining side right side up. Place the second lining piece on top of the stack right side down. Align the sides; align the top edges of the unsewn rectangles with the top edge of the zipper. Pin and sew next to the zipper teeth as before.

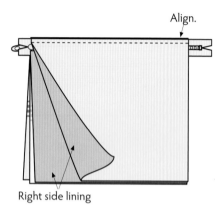

Align.

Right side lining

4 Flip the lining and toweling over so the wrong sides are facing each other and press along the sewn edge.

5 Open up the layers. Position the two lining pieces with right sides together and the two toweling pieces with right sides together. Pin all the way around.

6 Unzip the zipper enough so that your hand will fit through the opening easily. You might need to remove a couple pins to do this. Replace any pins and sew the layers together using a ¼" seam allowance, beginning at the bottom of the lining. Sew around all the sides and over the zipper; leave a 4" space at the bottom of the lining.

Leave open.

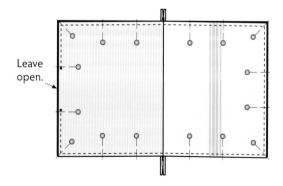

7 Cut off the zipper ends that extend past the ends of the fabric. Do not clip the corners or seams of the toweling, as it will unravel easily.

8 Before turning the bag right side out, bring the side and bottom seams together at the corner of the lining. Measure 1" from the point and draw a line perpendicular to the side seam. Sew along this line. Repeat on the opposite corner and then repeat with the bag exterior.

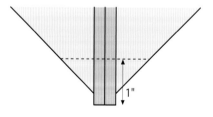

1"

9 Turn the pouch right side out through the opening in the lining. Sew the opening closed by hand or machine. Slip the lining to the inside through the open zipper. Close the zipper.

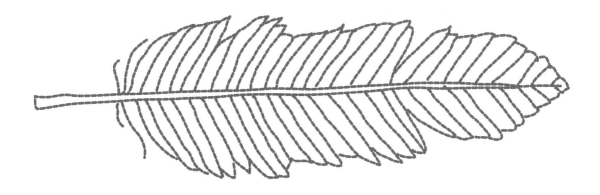

Overlapping seed stitches

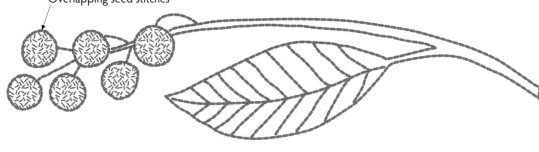

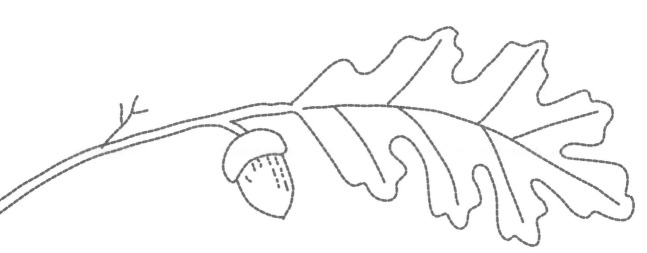

Embroidery key

------ Backstitch

Seed stitch

Embroidery Basics

In this section, you'll find some of the basic information you'll need for hand embroidery. If you're new to sewing and quilting, you can find additional helpful information at ShopMartingale.com/HowtoQuilt, where you can download free illustrated how-to guides on everything from rotary cutting to binding a quilt.

Quilt as Desired

I find it easiest to quilt through as few layers as possible, so I don't put a backing fabric under the batting. I never use a hoop, but I do baste the batting and embroidered piece together well. If it's a small project, I just baste around the outside. If it's larger, like Hazel (page 40), I baste a grid every 3" or so.

I have a hard time using a thimble, so I usually end up with sore fingers. Sometimes I'll use one of the stick-on "thimbles," and that works well for me. I think the most important thing is to enjoy the process and not get too caught up in the technical aspects.

Tracing the Design

When it comes to tracing or transferring the embroidery design onto your fabric, I recommend using a light box. Start by pressing the waxy side of a piece of freezer paper to the wrong side of the fabric. The freezer paper will stabilize the fabric and make tracing easier. Tape the design in place on the light box, and then center the fabric on top of the design and secure it in place. I like to use a Pilot FriXion pen to trace lightly over the design. (The ink in a Pilot FriXion pen will disappear with the heat of an iron.) A fine-point washable marker, a ceramic pencil, or a mechanical or wooden pencil with a fine, hard lead will also work. When tracing onto a dark fabric, a white chalk pencil works well.

If you don't have a light box, you can tape the design to a window or use a glass-topped table with a lamp underneath.

About the Fabric

One of my favorite background fabrics for embroidery is Moda Crackle. It has a subtle design that creates a lovely texture next to the embroidery stitches. I used this for the background of most of the projects in this book.

Needles

I'm often asked what kind of needle I use for embroidery. There are many types of hand-sewing needles, each designed for a different technique. Needle packages are labeled by type and size. The larger the needle size, the smaller the needle (a size 1 needle will be longer and thicker than a size 12 needle). An embroidery needle is similar to a Sharp, but with an elongated eye designed to accommodate six-strand floss or pearl cotton. You may want to try a size 7, 8, or 9. To be honest, for me the eye of the needle just needs to be big enough to thread!

Hoops

Embroidery hoops are used to keep the fabric taut, but not tight, while stitching. Hoops are available in wood, metal, and plastic, with different mechanisms for keeping the fabric taut. Any type of hoop is fine, so take the time to find one you're comfortable with. I don't use a hoop, but if you'd like to use one I suggest trying a hoop that is 4", 5", or 6" in diameter to see what you prefer. Remember to always remove your fabric from the hoop when you've finished stitching for the day.

Embroidery Floss

All of the projects in this book were stitched using two strands of The Gentle Art floss unless otherwise noted. These beautiful hand-dyed threads will bring the rich colors of fall to your stitching. The conversion chart below will give you an approximate match to DMC floss, but because the floss from DMC isn't overdyed as The Gentle Art floss is, your project will have a different finished look.

THE GENTLE ART	DMC
Autumn Leaves	833
Burnt Orange	921
Cidermill Brown	3863
Cinnamon	434
Country Redwood	355
Gingersnap	3826
Grape Arbor	3740
Green Tea Leaf	3051
Moss	3011
Mulberry	3857
Mustard Seed	832
Old Hickory	830
Picnic Basket	801
Piney Woods	730
Pomegranate	3328
Raven	310
Ruby Slipper	3830
Tin Bucket	535
Toffee	780
Tomato	920

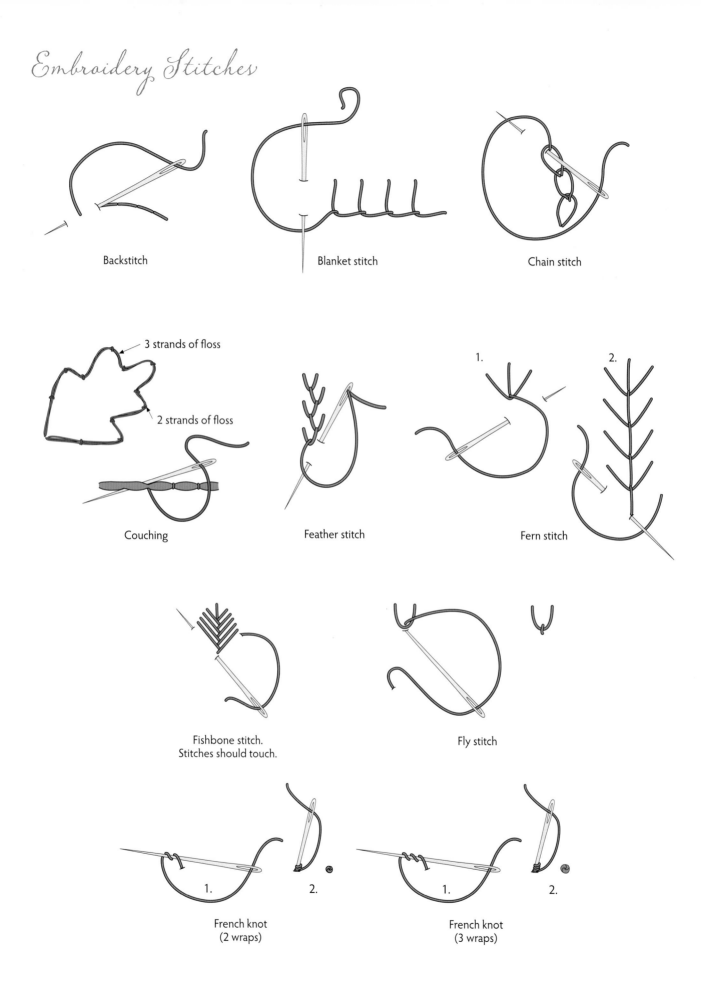

Backstitch

Blanket stitch

Chain stitch

3 strands of floss

2 strands of floss

Couching

Feather stitch

1.

2.

Fern stitch

Fishbone stitch.
Stitches should touch.

Fly stitch

1.

2.

French knot
(2 wraps)

1.

2.

French knot
(3 wraps)

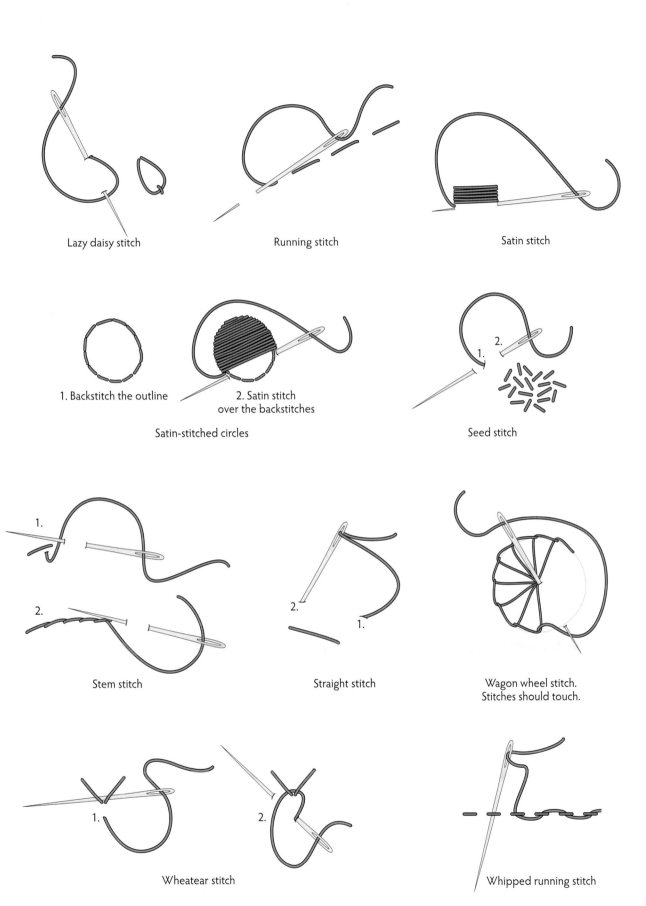

Lazy daisy stitch

Running stitch

Satin stitch

1. Backstitch the outline

2. Satin stitch
over the backstitches

Satin-stitched circles

Seed stitch

Stem stitch

Straight stitch

Wagon wheel stitch.
Stitches should touch.

Wheatear stitch

Whipped running stitch

Cord Making

Adding a simple handmade twisted cord to cover seams or to add a color accent can turn a sweet little project into a classic treasure. Some of the projects in this book are finished using cording made from six strands of floss and a cord maker. Using a cord maker is relatively easy and lots of fun.

1 Cut a length of floss following the project instructions. (Each project lists the length of floss needed to make your cording. The ratio of floss to finished cording is about 5:1.)

2 Tie the ends together to form a large loop. Place the knot end on the hook of the cord maker (fig. 1).

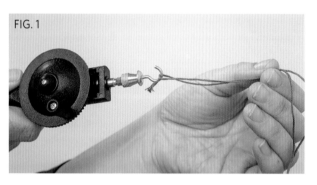

FIG. 1

Cording Tip

I make cording so often, I decided to screw a teacup hook into the side of my bookcase (fig. 2).

3 Attach the loop end of the floss to a hook or other stationary object and start winding (fig. 2). It's very important to keep the tension taut while winding. Just keep going! Remember, you must keep constant tension on the floss.

4 Do the "kink test" by keeping the cording taut and *slowly* bringing it closer to the hook on the cord maker. If the cording kinks and twists together, it's ready (fig. 3).

5 Keeping the tension taut, remove the end of the cording from the cord maker. Place the hook of the cord maker over the cording at about the center of its length. Keeping a grip on the cord maker, bring the two ends of the cording together with your other hand. Remove the other end from the teacup hook. Hold both ends in one hand, with the ends pinched together, and hold the cord maker in the other hand.

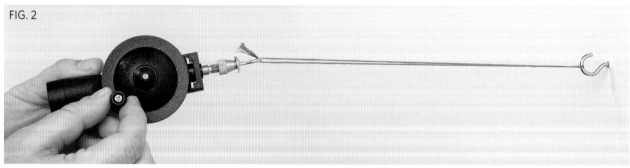

FIG. 2

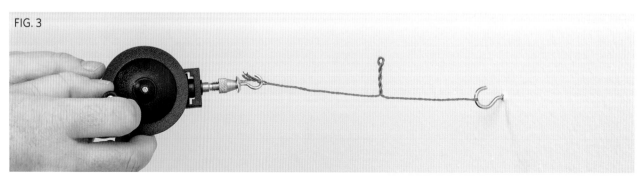

FIG. 3

6 Let go of the cord maker and let it spin and spin! When it stops spinning in one direction, remove it from the cording before it starts spinning in the opposite direction. Tie a knot at the ends you're holding (fig. 4).

FIG. 4

Resources
- -

Ackfeld Wire Stand
Available at craft stores or online:
www.AckfeldWire.com
I used item #87747 for Hazel on page 40 and #87607 for Welcome Home on page 60.

Cord Maker
www.KathySchmitz.com

Dunroven House Kitchen Towels
Miller's Dry Goods
4500 State Route 557
Millersburg, OH 44654
www.MillersDryGoods.com

The Gentle Art Floss
www.TheGentleArt.com

About the Author

When Kathy Schmitz was growing up, her mom always made sure that she and her sisters had an abundance of creative craft supplies at their fingertips. The girls were encouraged to draw and sew to their hearts' content, and many of their masterpieces were taped to the walls of their mom's sewing room. Kathy knew from a young age that *this* was what she wanted to do for a living! After many trials and errors, and jobs at banks and the like, Kathy says she is lucky enough to be what she always dreamed of being as a little girl—a designer. Kathy has designed fabric for Moda since 2002 and has had her

own pattern company since 2007. Put a needle and thread or pen and ink in her hand, and she's a happy camper!

Kathy lives in beautiful Portland, Oregon, with her sweet hubby of 32 years, Steve. Although her sons are grown and on their own, they are always close to her heart.